AFTERNOON TEA

To Make You Laugh. To Make You Cry - MY POETRY

BARBARA BURGESS

Crowfoot Publishing

AFTERNOON TEA

Poetry is what in a poem makes you laugh, cry, prickle, be silent, makes your toe nails twinkle, makes you want to do this or that or nothing, makes you know that you are alone in the unknown world, that your bliss and suffering is forever shared and forever all your own.

Dylan Thomas

To my family and to all who love poetry.

INTRODUCTION

I have been writing poetry since I was a youngster at primary school.

The earliest poem I remember writing is the one about the Whippet puppy.

I was probably about ten years of age when I wrote it.

I have had numerous poems published in local newspapers.

I love writing and especially poetry.

"Something might catch my eye, or someone might say something, and this will trigger off a thought process and the end result will be a poem."

CONTENTS

ABOUT - AFTERNOON TEA - THE POEM

AFTERNOON TEA – The First Poem in My Book.

Have you ever had one of those wonderful afternoon teas? We have had quite a few.

With family members in far off lands - Spain, Slovakia, Australia and spread far and wide in the U K - North, South, East, West and The Midlands - means that get-togethers do not come that often.

This poem is a reminder of a wonderful afternoon tea spent with family and exchanging late birthday, Christmas and other celebratory presents and moments.

Everyone's favourite on the menu was Chocolate Toffee Fudge Cake.

We always used to look for a restaurant that served Chocolate Toffee Creamy Fudge Cake.

AFTERNOON TEA

Meetings and greetings.
Crinkling wrapping paper.

Tapping of fingers.
Impatient.

Waiting to see the smile
That grows
On that glowing face.

Late presents given.
Birthday gifts,
Christmas too.

Coffee?
Don't mind if I do.

And oh, that rich dish,
Creamy Chocolate Toffee cake.

I cannot bake.
Fried egg my limit.
Maybe beans with it.

Today we dine
And spend precious time
Together

ABOUT - LITTLE WHIPPET PUP

This poem about a little puppy is one of the first poems I recall writing.

I wrote it about my Border Collie Sue who sadly had to be put to sleep when she was only four years old.

She had fits and the last fit she would not come out of.

It was a heart-breaking experience and I write about it in one of my other books – PSYCHIC PETS.

I was about eleven years old then and at senior school.

Sue ate a bar of soap once and she would gather up all our shoes and place them in the centre of the room.

She also loved to carry big sticks and the bigger the better. Some were so heavy she could hardly lift them.

Sue was my love, my life, my soul.

I was heartbroken when she died and in such a terrible manner.

The English teacher asked us to submit a poem for our homework and so I changed this poem a bit and made it about our Whippet puppy who was called Sherry.

The teacher enjoyed it very much.

LITTLE WHIPPET PUP

Four muddy feet,
And one wet nose.

A hole in the garden,
Where there should be a rose.

A cry outside.
A scratch at the door.

A tired dog, asleep,
Curled up on the floor.

Bones to chew.
Slippers as well.

What she'll find next,
We never can tell.

She doesn't like baths,
Loves a walk in the rain.

She's a little Whippet pup,
And Pip is her name.

Poetry is not a turning loose of emotion, but an escape from emotion; it is not the expression of personality, but an escape from personality. But, of course, only those who have personality and emotions know what it means to want to escape from these things.

T.S. Eliot

ABOUT - SOMEBODY'S DOG

My third poem in this book - SOMEBODY'S DOG – always makes me cry no matter how many times I read it.

This poem was written in about 1952 by my Great Uncle Joseph E. Shadbolt.

He moved from Eastbourne, Sussex to Massachusetts, USA.

He had many poems printed in the local newspaper and was well-known as a poet.

He often wrote to my brother and sent him a number of poems. One was all about what you can do with a handkerchief. However, that poem seems to have got lost along the way.

This poem cuts to the core and must have been written by someone who understands the relationship between dogs and humans.

SOMEBODY'S DOG

"Only a dog."
Said the cop on the street.
Only a dog,
That lay at his feet.

But one of God's creatures,
As such it was born,
Now victim of someone,
Who just honked his horn.

Only a dog.
Maybe a joy
Torn from the heart
Of a dog-loving boy.

Someone will feel
The pain and regret
A dog-lover knows
At the loss of a pet.

Someone will miss
The heart-warming hail
Voiced without words
By a dog's wagging tail.

In somebody's life
A dog plays its part.
A place of his own
In somebody's heart.

So, Mr Driver,
Wherever you are,
Please be more careful
When driving your car.

Just for a dog's
And for somebody's sake,
When tooting your horn
Bear down on the brake.

And Mr Policeman,
Whatever your name,
For a common expression,
You're not to blame.

But don't let a stock-word
Your good nature befog.
Please don't say, "only,"
Say "somebody's dog".

ABOUT - MISTY MORN

I was inspired to write the following poem – MISTY MORN - after taking my Border Collie out early in the morning.

I love the early mornings when no-one is around.

It seems to me there is a cut off time when all is quiet and then suddenly everyone wakes up and the roads are busy once more.

I saw several cats.

The nurse came to see to the elderly lady next door to us.

A chap was getting his van ready for work and he was bright and cheerful.

A lad rode his bike down the middle of the road and he was whistling.

Lovely to see and hear people being bright and cheerful first thing in the morning.

MISTY MORN

Misty morn,
Crack of dawn.

What's that I hear?
Nothing to fear.
Just cats in the ally.

Fighting, Biting,
Scratching, attacking.

Too late, their mate has run away.
Today no unwanted kittens.

That's a good thing.
The feline race is large enough.

Tough being a stray in the dark.
Sleeping rough in the park.

Creeping, stalking.

Walking the streets, the night long.

Till dawn birdsong.
Dark shadows 'neath a car.

A shape on a wall.
Tall, like a leopard.

No true big cats here.
Just shapes.

Shadows on the brickwork.
Lit by the glow from a lamp post.
Most people still a slumber.

"Dreadful day" someone mumbles,
As they creep back to their duvet-warm bed.

And the cat sits on the roof of the shed
Eyeing up his territory.

Oh glory, glory,
The sun begins to show her pretty face.
And the lace of cobweb dew shimmers in her
     light.

"Good night" says the duty nurse.
"A curse this topsy-turvy world.

Swapping night for day and day for night.
Not right.

Can I have a good sleep for once?
Feel like a dunce when tiredness robs me of my
     memory."

Still she gathers up a smile.
While the man with the van and his tools
Bids "good morn."

The lad on a bike gives a wave and a yawn.
And home once again.

The dog in his blanket entwined.
How quickly sleep he finds.

Me?
Hot tea.
My favourite blend.

ABOUT - OFF TO THE SHOW!

My husband Richard is a photographer. He enjoys street photography and is also interested in 1940s and other re-enactment events.

We decided to pop along to a Traction Engine show and Country Fair in Derbyshire, August 2019 and before we went, I wrote the following poem.

This was also at the time when I was on the 21 day Write from The Heart Group, organised by Wendy Fry. so I wrote about my day.

OFF TO THE SHOW!

Out of bed,
Sleepy head.

Where's my pen?
Gone again.

Want to write.
Hold tight - found it.

Dog peeps from under his eye lids.
A treat please, or I won't go out.

What's that on your feet?
Slippers, not walking shoes.

Not amused.
It's back to bed for me.
I want a tree to pee on!

Breakfast at last.

Break the fast.

Off to the show.
Let's go.

Busy day ahead.
Shed those towny cobwebs
With a day in the country.

Yipeeeeee!

ABOUT - THEY'RE PULLING THE HOUSES DOWN IN LUTON TOWN

I used to work in the centre of Luton, Bedfordshire, in a factory.

I have had many jobs. I once counted them and stopped counting at about thirty.

I went to work by bus and would sit and look out the window and daydream.

On one journey to work I noticed how the houses were being pulled down and then I saw blocks of flats being built.

I met a lady who was living in one of the blocks of flats and she told me how lonely and isolated she felt.

The town centre was also changing with shops being pulled down to make way for a new shopping centre.

I was also told that the company for which I worked was moving their business to another factory.

Hence the following poem came into my mind.

It was published in The Luton News. I think the headline was – 'she's a poet and she don't know it.' Or something like that.

THEY'RE PULLING THE HOUSES
DOWN IN LUTON TOWN

They're pulling the houses down in Luton town.
They're pulling the houses down in Luton town.
Dear old Auntie Pat
Now lives in a top-floor flat,
'Cos they're pulling the houses down in Luton
town.

They're pulling the old shops down in Luton
town.
They're pulling the old shops down in Luton
town.
Where I used to buy a bread roll
There's just a bloomin' great hole.
'Cos they're pulling the old shops down in Luton
town.

They're pulling the factories down in Luton
town.
They're pulling the factories down in Luton
town.

They said, 'no work today',
And gave me two week's pay.
'Cos they're pulling the factories down in Luton
   town.

Poetry is the opening and closing of a door, leaving those who look through to guess about what is seen during the moment.

Carl Sandburg

DANCING WITH DOLPHINS

DANCING WITH DOLPHINS - Inspired by my love of Dolphins
and swimming.

Dancing with Dolphins,
I fly through the air,
Then plummeting earthwards,
Splash waves everywhere.

Diving with Dolphins,
I cut through the blue,
As the dawn light reflects
Off my pewter-like hue.

Drifting with Dolphins,
I take life in my stride.
Each day is its own,
I wander oceanwide.

Dreaming with Dolphins,

I float in liquid bliss,
And from one aquatic giant,
Accept a gentle kiss.

Dancing with Dolphins,
I blend my energy,
As sounds vibrate within my soul,
Through ocean therapy.

MAGIC CARPET

MAGIC CARPET - A poem covering the seasons.

Carpet of leaves
If you please.
Oh, I don't know.

Carpet of frost.
Get lost!

Carpet of dew.
Now that's new.

Carpet of rain,
Down the drain.

Carpet of sunshine,
Yes, that's mine.

Carpet of rainbows
When out walking
Now you're talking.

ABOUT - AUTUMN LEAVES

The following poem – AUTUMN LEAVES - took me a long time to write.

I recall walking the dog and seeing the Autumn Leaves falling from the trees, and this was the beginning of the poem.

My mind then wandered about, and I pictured myself kicking up the leaves as a child. I also remembered the sound of crisp leaves being kicked up or crunched upon.

One memory was of walking along next to a flint stone wall in Eastbourne and kicking up the leaves there. I think the tall wall circumnavigated the Ocklynge Cemetery where many of my Chatfield and Shadbolt relatives are buried.

Each Autumn for a few years, the poem popped back up in my mind. What words to rhyme? How to lay the poem out?

It was not until I saw an Autumn poetry competition that I decided to complete the work.

It can never be perfect.

That is one thing I have learned – you do not have to be perfect.

In real life, nothing is perfect.

If you look.....

Trees, flowers, animals, humans, the weather – nothing is ever perfect, and so we do not need to strive for perfection in our creative endeavours.

Someone once asked how long it took me to write a book/ The answer can be from a weekend to years.

This poem was first written in 2005 and now published in 2019.

AUTUMN LEAVES

I kick up the leaves,
as I flick up my memories,
of days in the park,
and playing with friends
in the street after dark.

Crunch, 'neath my feet, crispy leaves.
still crisp are my memories.
of warm summer sun.
sand dunes and riding.
dogs on the run.

Softly falling, golden leaves.
still gold are my memories
of days by the sea,
dripping ice-cream,
sipping tea.

Stored away are pressed leaves.

in a box are my memories.
Precious moments, camera caught.
paper words, ribbon tied.
tucked in boxes, hid from view.
stored in archives of my mind.

In science one tries to tell people, in such a way as to be understood by everyone, something that no one ever knew before. But in poetry, it's the exact opposite.

Franz Kafka

ABOUT - ODE TO A SUPER DUPER POOPER SCOOPER

After moving around the county of Bedfordshire a few times, we decided to move to Lincolnshire.

We bought a smallholding not far from Skegness.

It was in the middle of nowhere down a long-unmade track, and yet it was quite near the town for shopping. You could easily walk to the shops, and sometimes we got on our bikes and went shopping.

We had numerous animals.

Pigs, sheep, ducks, pheasants, geese, chickens, turkeys and dogs and probably a few more besides. At one time we had some goats.

We reared our pigs outdoors and fed them organic feed. Someone said we were way before our time and no-one wanted outdoor reared, organic fed, meat.

People also complained to the RSPCA that our pigs were outside in the rain. When someone contacts the RSPCA, they have to respond to the call. The RSPCA person was very helpful. Our pigs continued to live happily outside.

We also had geese and as there were foxes around all the birds had to be shut in at night.

To begin with, the young geese did not mind, however, as they got older, they were harder to round up. They complained loudly at being herded into the large barn.

We bedded them on straw, and they stamped on it all night long. In the morning, it was easy to clean the building out as the stuff had turned into what I called 'sheet shit.' I used a shovel and could lift about one meter square of the stuff. It was a quick and easy job to clean their home.

If you have a pig in a sty, then all you have to do is put their food dish and water trough on the opposite side to the door. This way, they will poop by the door, and it is easy to gather it all up.

Having also bred and reared Whippet, Spaniels and other breeds of puppies then it is no wonder I know a lot about poo.

Puppies will eat anything and then they do a poo according to the colour of whatever it is they have eaten. Green toy, green poo. Orange cardboard box, orange poo, and so on.

One of my Whippets was in whelp and she must have had a craving for things just as some pregnant women do. She ate a long piece of thin cloth one day. I caught her with the tiny end bit sticking out of her mouth. I gave her loads of cod liver oil and the following day she began passing this roll of cloth. About a foot of it was sticking out of her bottom. I trod on this and as she walked away the other several feet of narrow cloth came away. Luckily she was fine and did not need to see the vet.

As you can imagine with so many animals, there was a lot of muck collecting to be done; hence.

I wrote this poem one day after cleaning up from a litter of pups.

ODE TO A SUPER DUPER POOPER SCOOPER

Oh, I am a great shit, shoveller.
Oh, I do love shovelling shit.
I'm an expert on the subject.
You should ask me about it.

I've seen it soft, I've seen it hard.
On the lawn and in the yard.
On the pavement, no that's wrong.
The neighbours do not like the pong.

I've seen it white and sometimes black.
I put it in my plastic sack.
Sometimes yellow. Sometimes green.
And even rainbow colours I've seen.

I run with my spade and scoop it up.
'No don't do that you mucky pup!"
I can train my dogs to sit and stay but not matter
　　what I do,

I simply cannot teach them how to use the
flipping loo!

THE HOUR BEFORE DAWN

A poem inspired by early morning walks with my dog.

Full moon so bright,
You light my way.

As I walk and talk
To my dog.

No fog,
Thank goodness.

Less noise and traffic,
Which pleases me.

Trees with singing birds
Perched on top.

They do not stop
As I pass by.

I hear a Cockerel cry.
A lovely sound.

Bound to wake someone
From their nightly slumber.

I remember many things.
My mind has wings.

In this quiet time.
The hour before dawn.

CAT ON A HOT TIN ROOF

There are cats everywhere when I walk my dog.

And the cat lays top o' garden shed.
On white paw rests tabby head.
Flashing lights, busy refuse collectors.
The morning postman delivers his letters.

And the cat gives a yawn, mouth open wide.
And the tiny mouse 'neath the shed goes to hide.
And the fish in the pond keep quite still.
Semi-hibernation with winter's chill..

And the cat looks up at the birds in the trees.
No butterflies to chase and no buzzing bees.
She'll just have to lie there a little bit longer,
'Til sun's day-warmth becomes a bit stronger.

And the cat's front legs she stretches out.
Now deciding the best thing is moving about.
She wanders to the edge of the garden roof,

And sits for a while staring, aloof.

And the cat gives a yawn and stretches again.
In the distance the sound of the morning train.
And the boy on his bike goes whizzing by,
And eerily she listens to the fox's distant cry.

And the cat she sits and looks around,
At the Blackbird singing – a wonderful sound.
And she lays on her back and stretches again,
Then twitches her ears as it starts to rain.

And the cat jumps off the garden shed,
And into the cat flap she runs for her bed,
And onto the sill from her perch on the sofa,
And stays there watching till night duties take
    over.

ABOUT - A SHOW DOG'S LAMENT

A SHOW DOG'S LAMENT – This poem is reminiscent of the time when I showed Whippets.

I used to show, and breed Whippets and I bred International and Nordic Champion Wellnigh Norseman of Dondelayo. Anne Knight of the Dondelayo Whippets saw how good he was, and she bought him off me.

I also trained Springer Spaniels to the gun and went to a Field Trial once only and came about sixteen out of eighteen. I was glad we did not come last.

I love breeding and showing animals and feel that I have an 'eye' for a good animal. I also love training dogs.

I am now too busy with my writing to follow any of the above pursuits anymore.

The following poem comes from when I showed a lovely bitch called Dondelayo Lynette. She behaved so badly in the ring. Her legs went everywhere, and she messed about. When we got out of the ring, she looked up at me as if to say, 'didn't I do well.' She was almost laughing! Hence the poem.

A SHOW DOG'S LAMENT

One Sunday we all went off to a show.
The judge said, "she's a beauty, you know.
Her shape is correct, and her movement is true.
You wouldn't sell her to me, would you?"

Well I won a cup, a card and some money.
And then she started to call me Honey.
She said that I was her favourite pet.
And better than me she'd not seen yet.

We sat all day outside the big ring.
Next to Crufts this is the thing.
Then in I went. A prize and a card.
She said that we'd do it if we worked hard.

Yes, she knew that we'd do it without any doubt.
And everyone clapped and friends gave a shout.
The judge looked at me. I'd won Best in Show!
It made her so happy her eyes were aglow!

She said I was elegant, graceful and classy.
Then looked away as her eyes went all glassy.
She said amongst thorns, that I was a rose.
Then wiped a tear from the tip of her nose.

And when it was over we got in the car.
She said she was glad that we didn't live far.
She said she would show me the next weekend
And during the week for some schedules she'd
    send.

I thought, "this is it, now she'll never stop talking
'Bout get me fitter, and that meant more
    walking!"
She gave me a bath and she brushed my hair.
I was beginning to think that it wasn't fair.

Then on Saturday morning she got me up early.
She had make-up on, and her hair was all curly.
With lunch and some blankets off we went.
But oh, it was awful, a show in a tent.

Well it rained and it poured, and I was froze.
And a big fat man stood on her toes.
And the judge said, "oh my word what a mess.
You're not telling me that this is your Tess?

Well her back is humped, and her head is down.
And look at that face! Never seen such a frown.
Her body's too short and she's got no stifle.
Get a new puppy dear. With this one don't trifle."

Well she said that she'd never felt so ashamed.
And it wasn't the weather but me that she
    blamed.
She said that I'd acted just like a clown

And she's seriously thinking of putting me down.

She that was it with showing she's through,
And she'd make enquiries 'bout me at a zoo!
Well I did feel hurt, but I wagged my tail.
And to top it all it began to hail.

And all the way home not a word was said.
But she did kiss me when she put me to bed.
And he could see she was near to tears
So, he cooked the dinner. He's not done that for
     years!

"Come on deary. Do cheer up.
I've brought you some tea in your favourite cup.
It's worth one more try." Well that's what he
     reckoned.
So, he took me, and guess what I got?
A second!

FULL MOON ABOVE

Poems can be short of long – here is a short one and composed at the time of – yes, you've guessed it – the full moon. In 2019 there were some rare full moons and eclipses.

> Full Moon above
> I love you

FULL MOON ON HIGH

Full moon on high,
Black sky frames you.

People blame you
For their madness

'Tis sadness.
For they cannot say,
Sunrise brings the blessed day.

THE HALF MOON

At the sign of the new Moon write your letter of wishes, desires, hopes
and dreams. At the sign of the full Moon then burn your letter to the
Moon and await your dreams to come true.

Half-moon aglow,
You show yourself.

Framed in the dark,
By the garden trellis work.

Do you know me?
I know you.

Always shining up there.
Never a care.

Radiant light,
By night.

Cool white by day.
You never cease to amaze me.

You are a constant in my life.
Reliable, trustworthy.

But sometimes hiding behind a cloud.
I call aloud.

"Moon where are you tonight?
Guide me with your light."

I send you full-moon wishes.
Lists of my desires,
And you answer my prayers.

Dare I ask for too much,
From a golden glowing light,
Such as yours?

MY LOVE

My love, my love,
Will you come to me?

I call you and you do not hear me.
I look for you and I do not see you.

I live in the dark.
No spark of your love can ever set me free.

MY LOVE

I am forlorn.
My love is gone.

I know not where.
I tug at my hair.
The pain eases my mind.

Pacing up and down.
I wander around,
And wonder where he is.

Is this the life I should lead?
Alone and lonely?

The days are so long.
The nights so dark.

The spark in my heart,
Went out long ago.

I sit and cry and sing
Lullabies that comfort me.

I feel like a child that would suck its thumb.
I am numb.

STRANDED

She walks down the aisle.
Talking nervously.

"Dad does my stomach show in this dress?"
What a mess, she thinks 'neath her smile.

Shotgun wedding.
Shock is the understatement.

At the altar she waits.
Nothing has altered.

He does not show.
What a blow, to her dignity.

Apologies to the vicar.
Someone in the congregation sniggers.

They gloat.
Best Man hands her a note.

Tears wet the paper.
Wishing they'd never met.

Feeling stranded.
Branded a single mum.

She strokes the white lace.
White face? Where can she hide it?

A grimace now shows.
Rows of relatives watching.

They see her anguish.
Wishes she could run away.

And outside in the cold it snows.
The blow has left her numb.

Dumb thing getting tangled up with him.
Head spinning. Eyes burning.

Left in the lurch, like others, no doubt.
"On yer bike," She thrashes out.

"And don't come back.
You lack love and responsibility."

She's left there. Stranded.
Can she sail away to some far-off land?

A deserted island.
And yet it's still a man she wants.

Someone to love her, care for her, keep her safe.
Embrace her when she is upset or hurt.

Not someone who will dish the dirt.
A reliable and trustworthy soul.

This is her goal.
As she walks, straight-faced back down the aisle.

"Dirty trick this guy has played on you."
"Yes, Mother, but what can I do?

I am like you.
Left at the altar,
Stranded.

ANOTHER LIFE TAKEN

Another life taken,
Flowers laid on a wall.

Another life taken,
Bouquets tied to a pole.

Another life taken,
A lamp post holds the sorrow.

Another life taken.
Flowers 'neath a tree the morrow.

MY COLLIE

My Collie rounds up sheep,
While he is asleep.

His paws rise up and down.
His face it wears a frown.

His whimpers can be heard,
Like the twittering of a bird.

Tiny yaps he utters,
As the eyelid flutters.

The sheep now in the pen,
He is awake again.

And finds himself at home,
No more in sleep to roam.

BLUSTERY DAY

Outside the wind does moan.
Inside we're safe and warm.

Copper beech does bend and groan.
He'll not come to harm.

Fearful dog does sit and quiver.
Hiding mice do snuggle and shiver.

On the window the rain she lashes.
Old fence to the ground it crashes.

The birds all hide away,
As the dawn meets this blustery day.

SNOWDROPS AND DAFFODILS

Snowdrops and Daffodils,
A beautiful sight.

Snowdrops and Daffodils,
Sent to delight.

'Though it is cold,
A sign of the Spring.

To warm on the inside.
And make our heart sing.

ANOTHER BLUSTERY DAY

The pines across the road sway.
Another blustery day.

The wind whistles through the window pain -
    again.

Branches fall
The pines stand tall.

Road-works signs.
Men drilling,
Filling holes.

Dog asleep,
After a meaty breakfast
And a lark in the park.

Sky dark,
And the pines still sway.
Another blustery day.

SILLY WORD

I've got a silly word here.
I made it up today.

The word is – jimblydimbly.
And it makes me laugh – hooray!

I say it when I happy.
I say it when I'm sad.

I say it when I'm good.
And I say it when I'm bad.

I say it all night long,
And in the daytime too.

If you say it with me,
Then I'll speak along with you.

Jimblydimbly, jimblydimbly,
Jimblydimbly do.

THINGS I LOVE

Clear blue sky.
Wispy clouds floating by.

Tall trees in a glade,
Giving me shade.

Balmy days.
Mist and haze.

Golden sand.
Seaside band.

Days of leisure.
Eating for pleasure.

Trips by train.
The sound of rain.

Puppy smell.
Church bell.

Buzzard cry.
Stoat running by.

Gentle breeze.
"Bless you," when I sneeze.

The first sign of snow.
The moon's glow.

Snowdrops, raindrops and dew.
Buttercups' golden hue.

Cowslips, parsnips, and carrots.
Guinea Pigs and Parrots.
Sheepdogs and cats.
Mice, snakes and bats.

Palm trees swishing.
Wells for wishing.

Time with friends, time alone.
Afternoon tea with cream scone.

Summer, Winter and Spring.
Just about everything.

The colours of day, the colours of night.
Stars in the heavens, shining bright.

The colours of fall.
I love them all.

SOCKS

Pink ones,
Blue ones.
Socks that don't match.

Holes in the heals.
Holes in the toes.

Darned socks.
Old ones.

New ones.
Smelly ones.

Wet ones the dog stole.
Warm ones the dog laid on.

Fresh from the line
Smelling sweet.
A treat for sore feet.

RUNNY NOSE

Always drip, dripping.
My runny nose.

Out in the countryside,
Wherever it goes.

Drips down my shirt.
Drips on my food.

Even a handkerchief
Is no good.

A drip makes me sneeze,
And sometimes cough.

You with a dry nose,
Yes, you can scoff.

For without this experience,
You'll never see,

How badly a dripping nose
Unpleasant can be.

STAND UP

Stand up for yourself.
Stand up for your rights.
You have choices.
You do not have to go with the flow.
You have your own mind.
Make it up – make it up now.
Do not follow others.
Follow your soul.
Your soul has rights.
Your soul has purpose.
Your soul is always whole,
No matter what anyone else has ever told you.
You are unique.
You are the only person with your talents.
No-one else on this earth
Has your combination of talents.
You are unique.
Stand up and make choices.
Do not allow others to make choices for you.
Make your own choices.

You can choose anything.
You can do anything.
You are a capable soul.
Many people have accomplished great things.
You are capable of accomplishing great things.
Do not be fooled by that inner voice that tells
you otherwise.
Do not listen to that inner voice.
That inner voice is just a replay of what you
heard before.
People telling you how useless you are.
People saying you cannot have this or that or the
other.
People saying you are worthless, no good.
Change that inner voice.
Tell it to stop.
Take a breath.
Breathe.
Relax.
Be calm.
Now tell yourself you are capable.
Tell yourself you can do whatever it is you want
to do.
You can do it now.
You have the choice.
Stand up.

THE SEASIDE

Sand 'neath my fingernails.
Sand up my nose.
Sand in my hair.
Sand between toes.

Salt in my ears.
Salt makes them ring.
Salt in my eyes.
Salt makes them sting.

Wind on my face.
Wind from the sea.
Wind warm embrace.
Wind cooling me.

A WALK IN THE WOODS

Arriving in the car park,
I get the dog out of the car.

Wondering which way to go,
I put on his collar and lead.

There are many paths.
Just as life has many paths.

I do not enjoy going there and back.
I prefer to do a circular route.

Today we take the muddy back path.
Ups and downs – just like life.

Harder to walk.
But what does that matter?

It makes me fitter,
Jumping over logs and dodging puddles.

I muddle through.
Around the twisted and exposed roots.

Life can make you feel exposed at times.
Life can make you want to hide in the woods at
      times.

Homeless are here.
Camping in a blue tent.

Nevertheless, a walk in the woods
Can easily still the mind.

I look up at the sky.
Clouds or clear – I do not mind.

I watch the leaves swishing in the breeze.
Pine trees creak in the wind.

Buzzards fly overhead.
Such a lovely call.

Like a messenger on high,
Saying, "I am here. I am looking after you."

A feather on the ground.
The angels are around.

Magic, Mystery, serenity.
Squirrels rush up the tree.

Toad stalls peep from beneath
The blades of grass.

Deer sometimes seen.
The thick trees make a safety screen.

A dog comes by.
Hello, goes his waggy tail.

The owner may or may not stop for a chat,
Or to pass the time of day.

Bikes go by slowly, or sometimes they whiz.
Quadbikes occasionally, a narrow miss.

Horses wait for us or we wait for them.
The Lakes, so calm and peaceful.

Ducks and Drakes.
Canada Geese.

A loan swan.
Where is his mate?

A coot or a few.
Drops of dew.

And it's full circuit.
Our walk in the woods.

Back at the car the dog takes a drink.
I think about our next walk.

THE HAPPY SONG

I've got a happy song,
And this song is just for you.

You can sing it all day long,
And in the night-time too.

You can sing it when you're smiling,
You can sing it when you're sad.

You can sing it if you're good.
And you can sing it when you're bad.

You can sing it in your head,
Or you can sing it right out loud.

Just sing along, all day long,
And be so very proud.

This song is such a happy song.
It makes me happy too.

I love my song, please sing along,
And you'll be happy too.

RAINBOWS

Rainbows.
I love them.

They make me feel warm and wanted.
They bring a smile to my face.

As if a prayer has been answered.
Angel grace.

High above.
Signs of love.

Full arcs.
Doubles when you are in trouble.

The light shining through,
Bringing wisdom to you.
Bringing answers of joy.

Where does the Rainbow begin?
Where does the Rainbow end?

How is a Rainbow made?
So many questions my friend.
But the Rainbow itself brings the answers.

Poetry can be dangerous, especially beautiful poetry, because it gives the illusion of having had the experience without actually going through it.

Rumi

ABOUT - FAUX PAS

Have you ever called a child by another child's name?

Worse still - have you ever called a child or any other person by your dog's name?

For some reason I manage to do this quite often.

Very upsetting and very embarrassing.

I recall my dad once said, "Goodnight Stephen." to me and I was very upset. I thought, my dad doesn't even know who I am.

But we can all make mistakes. And often we just say a name without even thinking.

FAUX PAS

Oh faux pas
You silly ass.

Did you do it deliberately?
Or did you lose your memory?

ABOUT - STONES - LIMERICK

My Limerick – STONES – was inspired by me being a Guild of Energists Energy Symbols Master.

We have stones and other items and we have twenty-three magical symbols that we paint on our stones and items.

We collect stones, you see, and sometimes it seems we have so many the floors will collapse!

We also 'read' the stones - just as a psychic would read the Tarot.

STONES - A LIMERICK

There once was a lady with stones
Who read them instead of the bones.
She placed them on boards
And in cupboards hid hoards
Now the floorboards give nothing but groans.

FINALE

Finale

CAT ON THE WALL

Cat on the wall.
Tall.

ABOUT THE AUTHOR

Psychic Medium

Medical Intuitive

GoE SuperMind Master

GoE Money Course

GoE Energy Symbols Master

Reiki and Seichem Master

Writer

Teacher

Chat Magazine

Author of books, ebooks and courses

Member of the Guild of Energists (GoE)

WHO I AM WIFE, MOTHER, ANIMAL LOVER

I am a wife to Richard and mother to Larissa and Selena. I am now a doting grandmother as well, to Skye.

NB. Baby Leo is due in September 2019.

I love dogs, although as a very young child I was petrified of them. I have owned, bred, shown, trained and judged Whippets, Gundogs, Terriers, Border Collies and other breeds and bred the Whippet International, Nordic Champion Wellnigh Norseman of Dondelayo.

I love working with dogs and training them. I have had many jobs – worked for British Rail as an office clerk, telephonist, and have even been a cleaner when my children were very young. I have also worked at Whipsnade Zoo and at Lincolnshire Shire Horse Centre.

To date I have written fourteen books and have contributed to one other. I have also created a number of courses. I have loved to write for as long as I can remember. I wrote my first manuscript when I was about ten and sent it off to a publisher.

I have my own publishing company - Crowfoot Publishing.

I also write film scripts.

WHAT I DO

I AM A PSYCHIC MEDIUM, ANIMAL COMMUNICATOR AND HEALER AND MODERN ENERGIST.

As Silvia Hartmann wrote as I was preparing this book of poetry - "We spread more LOVE around the world.

I consider myself to be a caring and considerate empath. I am an expert romance and relationships psychic. I also help people with money worries, businesses problems and family life or work issues.

I produce courses for people who wish to develop their psychic skills further. I coach people to a better way of life. I give help, guidance and advice to people who want to write books and get published. I work with the Angels and Spirit Realms to bring messages of joy and upliftment. I also give Mediumship Readings to those who wish to receive messages from loved ones and animals who have departed. I am also a writer and have my own publishing company – Crowfoot Publishing – I have written about 13 books to date. I write as Barbara Burgess and a pen name – Sarah Dunkley.

MORE ABOUT ME

Based in Kirkby in Ashfield, near Mansfield in the Nottinghamshire area, Barbara gives her expert readings to people locally and world-wide. Barbara has all the gifts of psychic ability.

Here are some, to name but a few:-

Clairvoyance – 'seeing with your mind's eye' – however I have sometimes seen spirit 'for real'.

Clairscentience – 'sensing spirit' – I sense spirit around me and also can sense other people's feelings and emotions. Claircognizance – 'just knowing' – I 'just know' what is wrong or what is happening around a person. Clairaudience – 'hearing within your mind' – I can also 'hear for real' so to speak, but not very often.

Mediumship – connecting with people and animals who have passed over to the other side. Proving that we live on in the spirit world.

I have always been interested in the mind. Whilst still at school I read **'Silva Mind Control'** by Jose Silva and learned how to send my mind places. This is called remote viewing.

However, like many people I have met since, I still did not think of myself as being psychic at all. I just felt I was 'improving my mind'. I was giving it exercises to do. Later on, in my twenties I read books by Betty Shine, Mind to Mind and her other books. They fascinated me.

These books also helped me to develop my psychic abilities further. Yet I still did not believe that I could do what other psychics could do. The ones I had seen on television. I was amazed that they could read tarot cards and give out messages to people.

It was not until I went to evening classes at Luton College of Further

Education and attended the Tarot and Clairvoyance courses with tutor Phil Griggs, that I actually realised that I was psychic after all and had been all my life!

You see, as a very young child I often smelled this strange perfume. It would turn up from nowhere. I somehow felt comforted whenever it showed up. I did not understand that I was clairscentient. I saw ghosts from a very early age and was not frightened by them at all. This meant that I had the gift of clairvoyance. There were often times when I 'just knew' something about someone or that something was going to happen or had happened. This means that I was and still am claircognizant.

I thought I knew what this was all about, but at the same time did not understand. I sometimes felt very different from my friends and was often bullied at school. Other psychics and sensitives that I have spoken to can tell similar stories to mine. I studied well at school. Did my homework. Was not one for partying and I was very shy and sensitive. A 'sensitive' is another word for a 'psychic'. Later on I went on many courses and workshops, such as Reiki Healing and Heal Your Life and these courses and workshops helped me develop my psychic abilities even further. I also developed my mediumship at Luton Spiritualist Churches and other churches in the various counties in which I lived.

My Paternal Grandparents are psychic, as are my parents. I believe I have inherited their gifts. My paternal grandfather read tea leaves and my paternal grandmother predicted the future with great accuracy. My parents are not really aware of their psychic abilities and yet I can see that they have them. My father loves to watch game shows on the t.v., the kind where you 'open the box' and get the millions of pounds. He invariably chooses the right box!

My mother has prophetic dreams and can sense spirit around her. My mother once dreamed of three cats. We used to have big, white fluffy cats. She dreamed of two white ones and a ginger one. Now a ginger cat is generally male. I have a brother and a sister. With hindsight my mother's dream was a warning. In the dream, one of the white cats was burned from its middle to its tail. A few days later I fell on a fire and had first, second and third degree burns from my waist and to the backs of my legs. I am a Psychic Medium, Angel Communicator, Clairvoyant, Medical Intuitive, Shaman, Channel, Animal and Nature Communicator. I give Angel Readings, Past Life Readings, Spirit Guide Readings and Guardian Angel Readings as well as Coaching, Life Coaching and Tuition. My gifts cover all the 'clairs' such as clairaudiance, clairscentience, claircognizance and clairvoyance.

I AM QUALIFIED IN NUMEROUS HEALING AND OTHER MODALITIES: GoE Energy Symbols Master, GoE Money Course, SuperMind Master, Advanced Medical Intuition, Modern Energy Healer and Member of the Guild of Energists (GoE). Angelic Mediumship (Charles Virtue). Reiki and Seichem Master, EFT (Emotional Freedom Technique), Emo(Energy in Motion) , Clinical Hypnotherapy, Counselling, Clairvoyance, Animal Healing, Realm Reader with Doreen Virtue, FreewayCER, Tapas Acupressure Technique, Healing Lives, Achieving Dreams, with Louise Hay via Patricia Crane, Tutor, Practitioner of Meridian Energy Therapies and City and Guilds Adult Teaching.

The above courses have helped me to enhance my psychic and mediumship abilities and write books, and have helped me to create a wonderful life for myself.

BOOKS BY BARBARA ON AMAZON

BOOKS BY BARBARA

For books by Barbara visit my Amazon page.

Books under my pen name - Sarah Dunkley

Books under - *Pretty Creative* are also available on Amazon.

Please visit my website:

www.barbaraburgess.co.uk

Cover image by:

V C BOOK COVER DESIGN

Poetry is thoughts that breathe, and words that burn.

Thomas Gray

For permission requests, write to the publisher.:

Crowfoot Publishing

42 Forest Street

Kirkby in Ashfield

Nottingham

Nottinghamshire

NG17 7DT

England

©Barbara Burgess

hello@barbaraburgess.co.uk

www.barbaraburgess.co.uk

Printed in Great Britain
by Amazon

21813426R00062